ALL AROUND THE WORLD
NEW ZEALAND

by Kristine Spanier, MLIS

Ideas for Parents and Teachers

Pogo Books let children practice reading informational text while introducing them to nonfiction features such as headings, labels, sidebars, maps, and diagrams, as well as a table of contents, glossary, and index.

Carefully leveled text with a strong photo match offers early fluent readers the support they need to succeed.

Before Reading

- "Walk" through the book and point out the various nonfiction features. Ask the student what purpose each feature serves.
- Look at the glossary together. Read and discuss the words.

Read the Book

- Have the child read the book independently.
- Invite him or her to list questions that arise from reading.

After Reading

- Discuss the child's questions. Talk about how he or she might find answers to those questions.
- Prompt the child to think more. Ask: New Zealand is a country of islands. Have you been on an island before? What was it like?

Pogo Books are published by Jump!
5357 Penn Avenue South
Minneapolis, MN 55419
www.jumplibrary.com

Copyright © 2022 Jump! International copyright reserved in all countries. No part of this book may be reproduced in any form without written permission from the publisher.

Library of Congress Cataloging-in-Publication Data

Names: Spanier, Kristine, author.
Title: New Zealand / by Kristine Spanier, MLIS.
Description: Minneapolis, MN: Jump!, Inc., [2022]
Series: All around the world | Audience: Ages 7-10
Identifiers: LCCN 2020057150 (print)
LCCN 2020057151 (ebook)
ISBN 9781636900179 (hardcover)
ISBN 9781636900193 (paperback)
ISBN 9781636900209 (ebook)
Subjects: LCSH: New Zealand—Juvenile literature.
Classification: LCC DU408 .S64 2020 (print)
LCC DU408 (ebook) | DDC 993—dc23
LC record available at https://lccn.loc.gov/2020057150
LC ebook record available at https://lccn.loc.gov/2020057151

Editor: Jenna Gleisner
Designer: Molly Ballanger

Photo Credits: Nathan White Images/Shutterstock, cover; Konrad Mostert/Shutterstock, 1; Pixfiction/Shutterstock, 3; Matt Champlin/Getty, 4; Filip Fuxa/Shutterstock, 5; Dmitry Pichugin/Shutterstock, 6-7; JoshuaDaniel/Shutterstock, 8-9; SuperStock, 10; Richard A Wall/Shutterstock, 11; Jiri Prochazka/Shutterstock, 12-13l; Minden Pictures/Alamy, 12-13r; Gary Blake/Alamy, 14; Dan Santillo NZ/Alamy, 15; davidf/iStock, 16-17; NopparatK/Shutterstock, 18-19; Johner Images/Getty, 20-21; i viewfinder/Shutterstock, 23.

Printed in the United States of America at Corporate Graphics in North Mankato, Minnesota.

TABLE OF CONTENTS

CHAPTER 1
Two Big Islands.................................4

CHAPTER 2
Rare Animals..................................10

CHAPTER 3
Life in New Zealand..........................14

QUICK FACTS & TOOLS
At a Glance...................................22
Glossary......................................23
Index...24
To Learn More.................................24

CHAPTER 1

TWO BIG ISLANDS

Would you like to paddle through a **fjord**? You can in New Zealand! This country is in the Pacific Ocean. It is made up of around 600 islands!

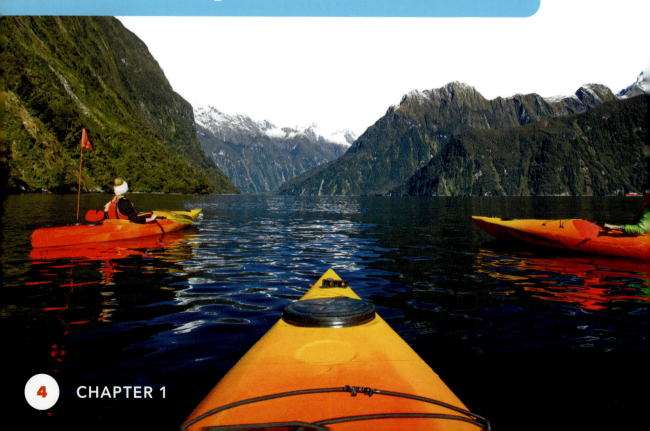

North Island and South Island are the two main islands. Frying Pan Lake is on North Island. It is one of the world's largest **hot springs**. The water reaches 140 degrees Fahrenheit (60 degrees Celsius)!

Frying Pan Lake

CHAPTER 1 5

The Southern Alps are a mountain range on South Island. Lupins bloom here from November to January. These flowers are pink, purple, blue, yellow, orange, and white. Some people travel here just to see them!

DID YOU KNOW?

Mount Cook is part of the Alps. It is the highest peak. It is 12,316 feet (3,754 meters) tall.

Most people live on North Island. Auckland has the largest **population**. Wellington is the **capital**.

The United Kingdom ruled New Zealand until 1907. It is now **independent**. A prime minister leads the government.

Wellington

TAKE A LOOK!

What do the parts of New Zealand's flag mean? Take a look!

UNITED KINGDOM'S FLAG: the relationship between New Zealand and the United Kingdom

BLUE: the color of the Royal Navy

STARS: the Southern Cross **constellation**

CHAPTER 1 9

CHAPTER 2
RARE ANIMALS

The waters around New Zealand are filled with marine **mammals**. Nine different **species** of dolphins live here. The Hector's dolphin is found nowhere else.

Hector's dolphin

The New Zealand fur seal is found on the rocky shores. These seals travel along rivers and streams. They sometimes show up in backyards!

The kiwi is a **symbol** of the country. New Zealand is this bird's only home. Even though they are birds, kiwis can't fly.

Kakapos also can't fly. These parrots only move at night. They can live to be 100 years old!

WHAT DO YOU THINK?

People here are called Kiwis. They are named after the bird. Is there a nickname for people where you live?

kiwi

kakapo

CHAPTER 2

CHAPTER 3
LIFE IN NEW ZEALAND

The Maori people lived here first. Many still follow Maori **customs**. They close their eyes and rub noses to greet one another. Many speak the Maori language.

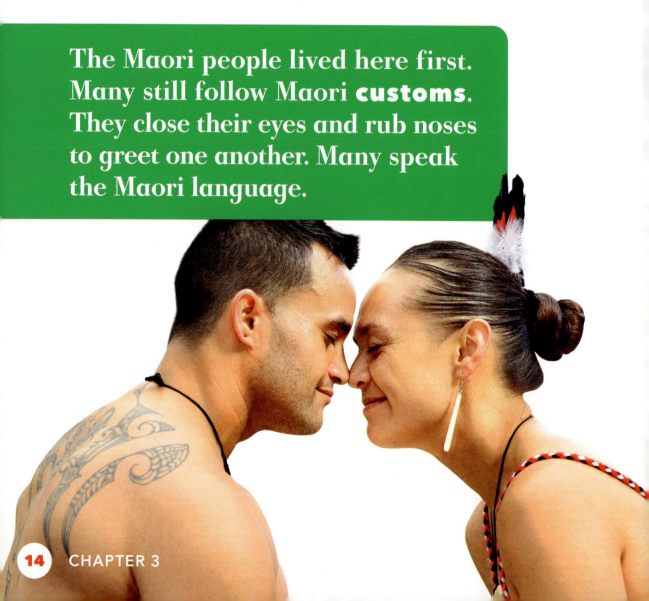

Hangi is a Maori dish. Meat, seafood, and vegetables are steamed in the ground.

hangi

Children go to school by the age of six. They attend until they are at least 16. Some go to private schools. Students who live in **remote** areas do online learning.

WHAT DO YOU THINK?

Boys and girls may attend separate high schools in New Zealand. Would you like to go to a school like this? Why or why not?

CHAPTER 3

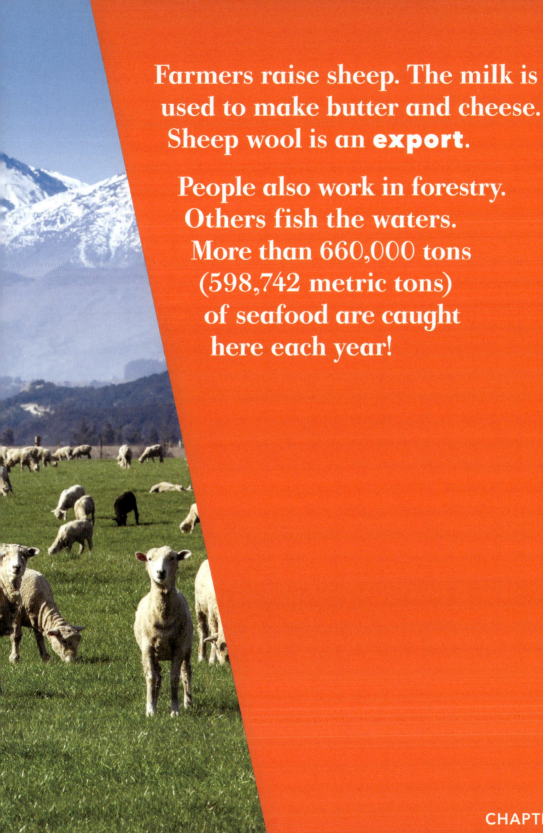

Farmers raise sheep. The milk is used to make butter and cheese. Sheep wool is an **export**.

People also work in forestry. Others fish the waters. More than 660,000 tons (598,742 metric tons) of seafood are caught here each year!

People in New Zealand love spending time outdoors. Hiking and climbing the mountains are popular. So is skiing. Many sail in the nearby waters.

There is much to discover in New Zealand. Would you like to visit?

CHAPTER 3

QUICK FACTS & TOOLS

AT A GLANCE

NEW ZEALAND

Location: South Pacific Ocean

Size: 103,799 square miles (268,838 square kilometers)

Population: 4,925,477 (July 2020 estimate)

Capital: Wellington

Type of Government: parliamentary democracy under a constitutional monarchy

Languages: English, Maori

Exports: dairy products, meats, logs, fruit, crude oil

Currency: New Zealand dollar

GLOSSARY

capital: A city where government leaders meet.

constellation: A group of visible stars that form a pattern when viewed from Earth.

customs: Traditions in a culture or society.

export: A product sold to different countries.

fjord: A long, narrow inlet of the ocean between high cliffs.

hot springs: Sources of hot water that flow naturally from the ground.

independent: Free from a controlling authority.

mammals: Warm-blooded animals that usually give birth to live babies.

population: The total number of people who live in a place.

remote: Far away, secluded, or isolated.

species: One of the groups into which similar animals and plants are divided.

symbol: An object or design that stands for, suggests, or represents something else.

New Zealand's currency

INDEX

Auckland 8
fjord 4
flag 9
forestry 19
Frying Pan Lake 5
hangi 15
Hector's dolphin 10
islands 4, 5
kakapos 12
kiwi 12
lupins 6
Maori 14, 15
mountains 6, 20
Mount Cook 6
New Zealand fur seal 11
North Island 5, 8
Pacific Ocean 4
prime minister 8
school 16
sheep 19
Southern Alps 6
South Island 5, 6
United Kingdom 8, 9
Wellington 8

TO LEARN MORE

Finding more information is as easy as 1, 2, 3.

1. Go to www.factsurfer.com
2. Enter "NewZealand" into the search box.
3. Choose your book to see a list of websites.